MAKERSPACE MODELS

BUILD YOUR OWN ROBOTS

Thanks to the creative team:
Senior Editor: Alice Peebles
Fact checking: Tom Jackson
Design: Perfect Bound Ltd

Hungry Tomato®
A division of Lerner Publishing Group, Inc.
241 First Avenue North
Minneapolis, MN 55401 USA

For reading levels and more information, look up
this title at www.lernerbooks.com.

Main body text set in Neutraliser Serif Regular 9.75/13.

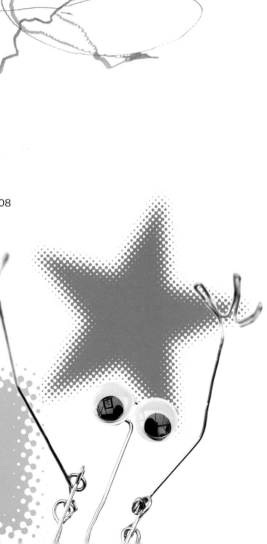

Library of Congress Cataloging-in-Publication Data

Names: Ives, Rob, author.
Title: Build your own robots / Rob Ives.
Description: Minneapolis : Hungry Tomato, [2018] | Series:
  Makerspace models | Includes index.
Identifiers: LCCN 2017046676 (print) | LCCN 2017058798
  (ebook) | ISBN 9781512498721 (eb pdf) | ISBN 9781512459708
  (lb : alk. paper)
Subjects: LCSH: Robots–Models–Juvenile literature. |
  Robotics–Juvenile literature. | Makerspaces–Juvenile
  literature.
Classification: LCC TJ211.2 (ebook) | LCC TJ211.2 .I94 2018
  (print) | DDC 629.8/92–dc23

LC record available at https://lccn.loc.gov/2017046676

Manufactured in the United States of America
2-46106-27698-5/22/2018

BUILD YOUR OWN ROBOTS

BY **ROB IVES**

HUNGRY TOMATO®
Minneapolis

SAFETY FIRST

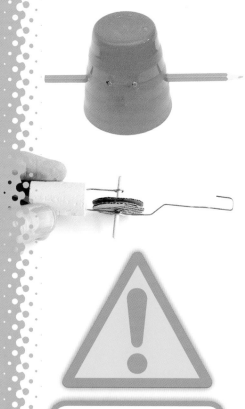

Take care and use good sense when making these fun model robots. They are all straightforward, but some activities call for cutting materials, drilling holes, and other skills for which you should ask an adult assistant for help (see below).

Every project includes a list of supplies that you will need. Most will be stuff that you can find around the house, or buy inexpensively online or at a local hardware or store.

We have also included "How It Works" for some models, to explain in simple terms the engineering or scientific principles that animate them. And for some there is a "Real-World Engineering" snippet that tells you more about the real-life versions of these projects.

Watch out for this sign accompanying some model instructions. You may need help from an adult with completing these tasks.

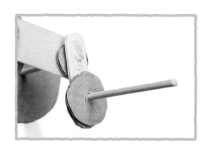

DISCLAIMER

The publisher and the author shall not be liable for any damages allegedly arising from the information in this book, and they specifically disclaim any liability from the use or application of any of the contents of this book. Readers should follow all instructions and warnings for each experiment in this book and consult with a parent, teacher, or other adult before conducting any of the experiments in this book.

CONTENTS

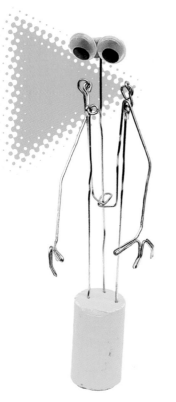

ROBOTS

Robots populate the big, wide world of science, technology, and space, right? They put cars together, carry out precise medical operations, and gather materials from remote planets to send back to Earth—among very many other things that are incredibly helpful to us humans.

There are also robots that are just fun to have around. Some even break records, such as the MultiCuber 999 that solved a 9x9x9 Rubik's Cube in 34 minutes 25.89 seconds!

So why not make your own? Here are eight cool ideas to try out, several of which mimic a human or animal equivalent, in true robot style. You can give your arm extra reach with a grabbing hand, set a mechanized insect skittering about, or get a doggie automaton nodding away.

If you don't like heights but love daredevils, get your tightrope performer to do the walking. Then enjoy some downtime as your penbot whizzes out some zany pictures—it could be the start of an interesting art collection.

So get your tools and materials together, start building, and see how these robots move. Your walking bot may not manage the 83.28 miles (134.03 km) achieved by Chinese robot Xinghzhe No. 1—but it's one mighty stomper!

TOP TIP

- Before you start on any of the models, read the step-by-step instructions all the way through to get an idea of what you're aiming for. The pictures show what the steps tell you to do.

- Some projects need pencils to be cut. Ask for help with this and use a cutting mat or similar surface to cut on. An efficient method is to cut each face of the pencil in turn with a utility knife, then snap the pencil apart. Tidy up any unevenness with the knife.

- You will need to connect a motor and battery to make some of your robots go. Do this by joining the end of one motor wire to the positive terminal on the battery and one to the negative terminal. On a cylindrical battery, the terminals are at either end. On a button battery, they are on either side. If in doubt, ask for help!

TOOL KIT

- Utility knife
- Long ruler or tape measure
- Electrical tape
- Wide double-sided tape
- Compass
- Gaffer tape (or duct tape)
- Epoxy glue
- Wire cutters
- White glue
- Craft drill
- Hot glue gun
- Clothespins
- Cutting mat
- Needle-nose pliers
- Kitchen scissors

EPOXY

WHITE GLUE

INTREPID EGGSPLORER

Add a rubber band to an egg, and you have a mini machine on a mission to discover the world. And if you want to keep up, better get in a good breakfast—eggs, perhaps?

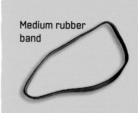
TOOLS:
- Needle-nose pliers
- Kitchen scissors
- Craft drill
- Wire cutters
- Hot glue gun (or plastic glue)

1 Use pliers to bend the wire into a double U-shape that is slightly narrower than the width of the plastic egg.

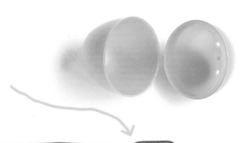

2 Use kitchen scissors to cut a small notch in each half of the egg at the join. Repeat on the opposite side. When fitted together, this makes two holes.

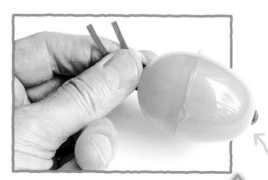

3 Drill two 0.1-in. (3 mm) holes at each end of the egg, 0.1 in. (3 mm) apart. Thread the rubber band through one end of the egg and out through the other end.

8

4 Tie the rubber band closed, so it's tight.

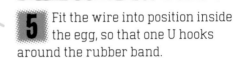

5 Fit the wire into position inside the egg, so that one U hooks around the rubber band.

6 Use wire cutters to bend the wire to make two small legs. Trim off any wire that extends beyond the end of the egg.

7 Use a hot glue gun or plastic glue to stick the eyes in place as shown.

8 Wind the legs around several times to twist the rubber band, and release.

TAKA-TAKA!

Your eggsplorer will race frantically across the floor!

HOW IT WORKS

Energy stored in the rubber band is released to create **kinetic energy.** Elastic is a special material that pings quickly back to its original shape when it has been stretched. This makes it a great exercise tool.

ROBOCRAWLY

You've probably noticed how fast insects run—for their size. Make this motorized bug and introduce it to your resident house spider. Maybe they could race each other!

YOU WILL NEED:

Double-sided sticky foam pads

Thin electrical wire, 4 in. (100 mm) long

Small pager motor

Three small paper clips

LR44 button battery, 0.4 in. x 0.2 in. (11 x 5 mm)

TOOLS:

- Needle-nose pliers
- Ruler
- Epoxy glue or hot glue gun
- Wire cutters
- Electrical tape
- Scissors

1 Straighten out the paper clips with the pliers. Bend 0.8 in. (20 mm) of the clips (0.4 in. [10 mm], doubled) into a narrow loop in the center of each.

2 Arrange the loops together and glue them with Epoxy or a hot glue gun.

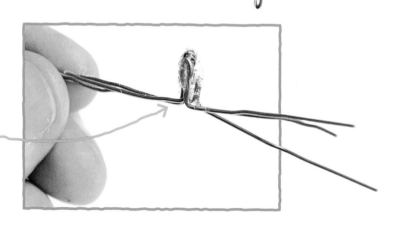

3 Cut two 2-in. (50 mm) lengths of wire. Expose the ends. Twist the end of one wire onto the end of one of the pager motor wires. Cover with electrical tape (not shown).

4 Cut a small square of sticky foam pad. Peel off one side and attach the exposed end of the other pager motor wire to the bottom of the battery.

5 Bend the wire loops back. Peel off the other side of the sticky pad and attach the battery on top of the wire loops. Shape the wires into three pairs of legs, as shown.

Glue the pager motor at the front for Robocrawly's head.

SKITTER!

6 Fold the free wire over and stick it to the top of the battery with another sticky pad. This sets Robocrawly going!

HOW IT WORKS

The pager motor vibrates and makes Robocrawly skitter about on the tabletop! This happens when the spare wire from the motor is connected to the battery to complete the **electrical circuit**, so the current flows.

TERMINATOR HAND

Our very nimble fingers and thumbs do lots of jobs for us, all day, every day. Now you can give yourself an extra-dextrous extremity: your very own robo-hand.

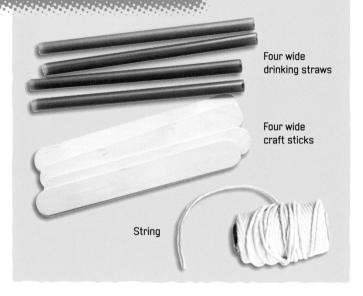

Four wide drinking straws

Four wide craft sticks

String

TOOLS:
- Utility knife
- Long ruler or tape measure
- Scissors
- Gaffer tape (or duct tape)
- Hot glue gun or Epoxy glue

1 Use a utility knife to cut three notches in the straws, the first 1 in. (25 mm) from one end, then 1.2 in. (30 mm) apart. They should have about a 45 degree angle and be cut more than halfway into the straw.

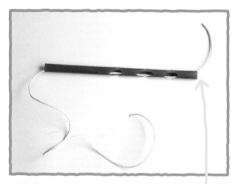

2 Thread a 20-in. (500 mm) length of string through the straw.

3 Fold the end of the string over at the notched end and secure with a small piece of gaffer tape. This is one finger—pull the string to test how it curls!

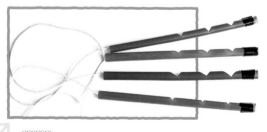

4 Make up three more fingers in the same way.

5 Glue the four fingers in place across a craft stick using hot glue or Epoxy. They should be angled slightly, about 0.2 in. (5 mm) apart at the base, then spreading out. The two middle ones extend a bit farther, like real fingers.

6 Pull the strings out through the lowest notches. Use a utility knife to trim the straws and the craft stick to length, as shown. Slot the strings back in place.

7 Glue a second craft stick under the first to make the wrist. Tie the four strings together. Trim three of the ends and tie a loop in the remaining end.

CRRUNCH!

Pull the loop to close the hand and pick up objects. Prepare to take over the world!

HOW IT WORKS

The notches allow the robot fingers to bend, like the joints of a real hand. Our hands each have 27 bones, arranged perfectly to work with tendons and muscles. That's why they move in so many clever ways. Scientists are developing soft robotic hands to mimic real ones, for use in medicine and as **prosthetic hands**.

TIGHTROPE TRICKSTER

Amazing highwire acrobats walk backward, blindfolded, and across huge drops. They even ride bikes up there! Get ready for some great stunts with this cool tightrope act.

TOOLS:
- Compass
- Ruler
- Utility knife
- White glue
- Clothespins
- Wire cutters
- Needle-nose pliers

YOU WILL NEED:

String

Different sized googly eyes

Scrap of corrugated cardboard

Two large and two small paper clips

One 1.2-in. (30 mm) washer, two 1-in. (25 mm) washers

Wooden skewer

Craft cork

1 Mark out four cardboard discs: two 1.6 in. (40 mm) and two 1.8 in. (45 mm) in diameter. Cut them out with a utility knife. Pierce the centers with the skewer.

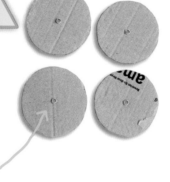

2 Thread the discs onto the skewer, placing the smaller discs in between the larger ones. Glue them together with white glue, and clamp with clothespins until the glue dries.

3 Trim the skewer with a utility knife or wire cutters to 0.8 in. (20 mm) on each side of the wheel, to complete the axle.

4 Use pliers to shape one long paper clip, including a raised loop, as shown, top right. Straighten the other long paper clip, make a matching loop at the end, and cut it to length with wire cutters. Both loops should be about 2 in. (50 mm) from the end.

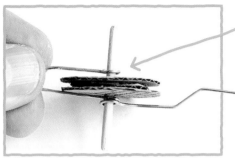

5 Slot the wire loops over the axle on either side of the wheel.

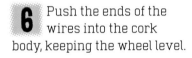

6 Push the ends of the wires into the cork body, keeping the wheel level.

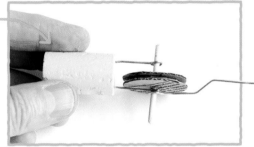

7 Use pliers to straighten out the two small paper clips and make arms and hands pointing in opposite directions.

8 Hang two or three washers from the end of the long wire. You'll need to experiment to find how many washers you need to keep the robot upright.

9 Push the arms into position just above the center of the cork, with one facing forward and one facing backward.

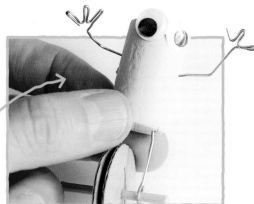

10 Glue two googly eyes to the top edge of the cork with white glue.

11 Tie one end of a length of string to a fixed point, such as a door handle, and hold the other end. Hook the robot onto the string.

WHEEEE!!

Raise and lower the string to make the robot scoot up and down!

REAL-WORLD ENGINEERING

The washers lower the robot's **center of gravity** and keep it upright. In real life, tightrope walkers often carry a pole or other horizontal balancing object. This lowers their center of gravity below the wire. The pole spreads out the body's mass and helps to maintain **rotational inertia**: that is, it opposes the wire's tendency to rotate and tip the walker. Skilled performers can do funny or clever tricks at the same time.

PAPER CLIP POWER

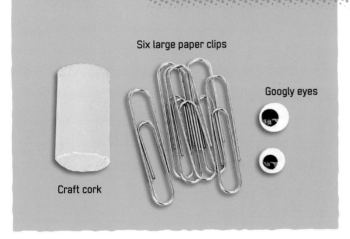

Six large paper clips

Googly eyes

Craft cork

Combine a few paper clips in a certain way, and you have a mini humanoid with working arms. Plus, the googly eyes will follow you around the room—see who blinks first!

TOOLS:
- Needle-nose pliers
- Epoxy glue

Arm (x 2)

Stand (x 2)

1 Use pliers to unfold four paper clips and shape two arms and two stands, as shown. The arms have a flat loop near the end and a raised one right at the end.

2 Hook the stands inside the inner loops on the arms.

3 Push the ends of the stands evenly into the cork.

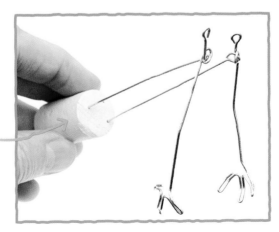

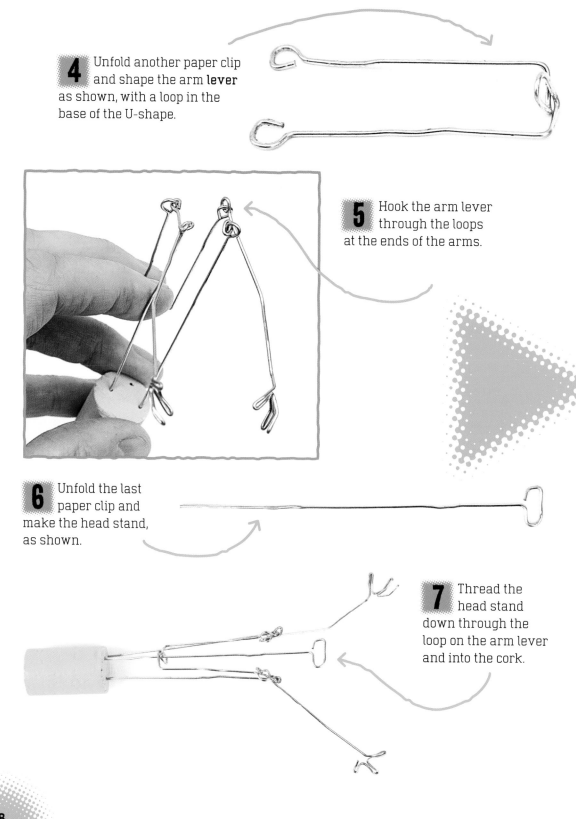

4 Unfold another paper clip and shape the arm **lever** as shown, with a loop in the base of the U-shape.

5 Hook the arm lever through the loops at the ends of the arms.

6 Unfold the last paper clip and make the head stand, as shown.

7 Thread the head stand down through the loop on the arm lever and into the cork.

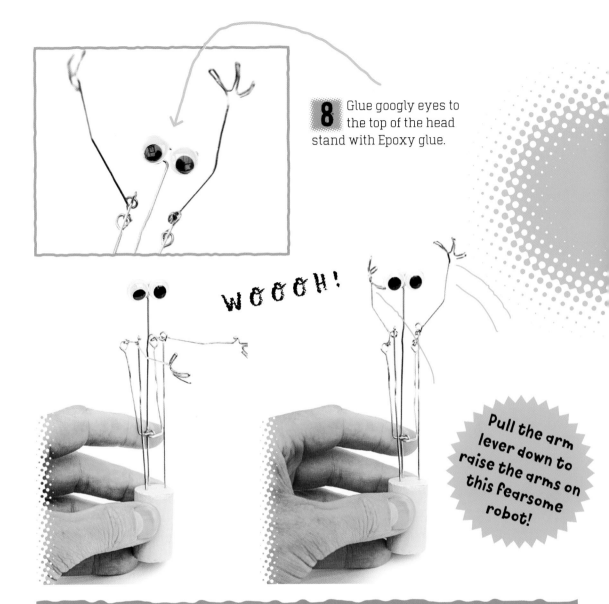

8 Glue googly eyes to the top of the head stand with Epoxy glue.

WOOOH!

Pull the arm lever down to raise the arms on this fearsome robot!

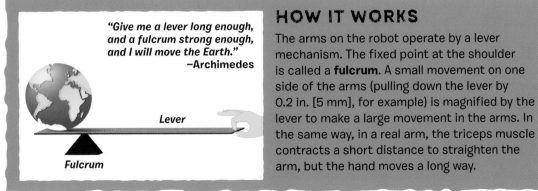

"Give me a lever long enough, and a fulcrum strong enough, and I will move the Earth."
—Archimedes

Lever

Fulcrum

HOW IT WORKS

The arms on the robot operate by a lever mechanism. The fixed point at the shoulder is called a **fulcrum**. A small movement on one side of the arms (pulling down the lever by 0.2 in. [5 mm], for example) is magnified by the lever to make a large movement in the arms. In the same way, in a real arm, the triceps muscle contracts a short distance to straighten the arm, but the hand moves a long way.

ROBODOG

What's great about this pet is that she doesn't need feeding or walks, but she's always there to amuse you and your pals! Not so ruff, is it?

TOOLS:
- Ruler
- Wide double-sided tape
- Compass
- Scissors
- Needle-nose pliers
- Wire cutters
- Craft drill
- Hot glue gun
- Cutting mat
- Epoxy glue

YOU WILL NEED:

Corrugated cardboard

Plastic cup

Pencil

Large paper clips

Googly eyes

Kitchen foil

Two craft corks

Small nut

1 Stick about 2.4 in. (60 mm) of double-sided tape to the back of a piece of foil. Cut out a foil circle 0.4 in. (10 mm) wider than the end of the cork.
Peel off the tape back and stick the circle to the cork. Cut out tabs from the excess tape and fold them down. Repeat at the other end.

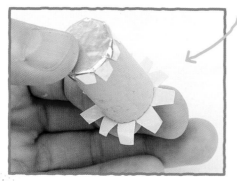

2 Cut a piece of double-sided tape the same width as the cork's height and long enough to wrap round the cork. Stick it to some foil.

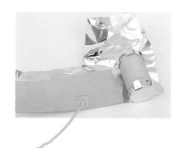

3 Wrap the foil around the cork. This is the head. Repeat steps 1–3 to make the body.

4 Cut a circle of sticky-backed foil to cover the end of the head, extending into foil-only dog ears. Stick in place on the head.

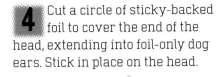

1.2 in. (30 mm)

5 Use pliers to make these wire pieces from an unfolded paper clip.

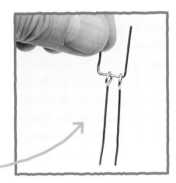

6 Thread the loops into the U-shaped staple.

7 Push the staple into the lower part of the head, as shown.

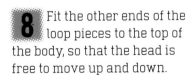

8 Fit the other ends of the loop pieces to the top of the body, so that the head is free to move up and down.

9 Unfold another paper clip and make the push rod pieces, as shown. The rod is 5 in. (130 mm) long, including the hook. Cut off a 2-in. (50 mm) piece for the staple.

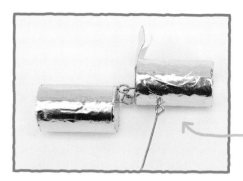

10 Slot the loop on the push rod over the staple and push the staple into the head.

11 Use pliers to straighten out two paper clips. Cut them into four 2.4-in. (60 mm) lengths. Shape four legs, as shown, and a straight tail with a curl at the end (*below*).

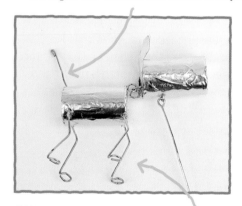

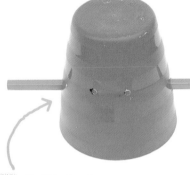

12 Fit the legs under the body and the tail on top.

13 Drill holes in opposite sides of the cup, halfway down, to fit the pencil easily. Drill two smaller holes in between and 0.6 in. (15 mm) above these. They should be 0.5 in. (12 mm) apart.

14 Cut out a roughly rounded cardboard plate, as shown. Make a paper clip staple about 0.8 in. (20 mm) long, to fit through the small holes in the cup. Push the staple through the cup and into the cardboard corrugations. Leave a loop so the plate dangles.

15 Perch the dog on the cup and mark where the feet will go. Drill a small hole between the front feet positions. Add a dot of hot glue to each footmark, then fit the dog in place.

16 Tape the push rod from the head to the front of the plate. Cut the pencil so that it is 1.6 in. (40 mm) longer than the cup width.

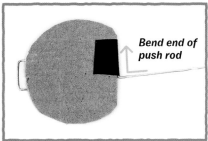

Bend end of push rod

17 Make a **cam** from a 1.4-in. (35 mm) circle of cardboard, with a pencil-sized hole 0.2 in. (5 mm) off-center. Thread the pencil into the cup and through the cam. (The plate sits on the cam to create the movement.)

19 Stick or glue on two googly eyes, and a nut for a nose with Epoxy glue.

W O O F !

18 Make a 1-in. (25 mm) cardboard washer. Add it to the left end of the pencil as the dog faces you (*see below*). Straighten a paper clip and wrap one end around the right end of the pencil. Shape the rest into a handle.

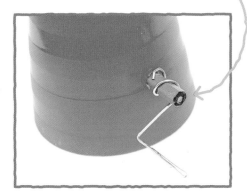

Turn the handle and Robodog will nod her head!

HOW IT WORKS

The dog is a simple **automaton** that uses a cam (a rotating piece) to make the dog nod. An automaton is a machine that brings a figure or scene to life through mechanisms. Some automata are complicated and can fire a bow and arrow or write a sentence!

PERFECT PENBOT

YOU WILL NEED:

Time to get creative with your own robo-artist. Connect up the motor and see the patterns flow from the marker tips—no two designs will be the same!

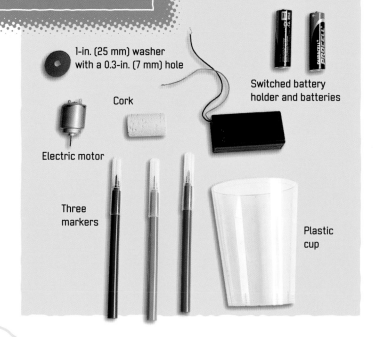

1-in. (25 mm) washer with a 0.3-in. (7 mm) hole

Cork

Switched battery holder and batteries

Electric motor

Three markers

Plastic cup

TOOLS:
- Craft drill
- Hot glue gun
- Utility knife
- Gaffer tape (or duct tape)

1 Fit the batteries into the holder. ⚠️ Make a small hole in the bottom of the cup with a craft drill and thread the wires through the hole.

2 Glue the battery holder to the inside of the cup near the top, using a hot glue gun. ⚠️

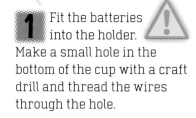

3 Use a utility knife to cut off a 0.4-in. ⚠️ (10 mm) section of cork.

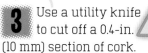

4 Press the cork piece onto the motor spindle.

6 Tape three markers, evenly spaced, around the cup with gaffer tape, so the tips extend about 1.2 in. (30 mm) beyond the top.

5 Use the hot glue gun to attach the washer to the cork so that it is just off center.

7 Leave the caps on until you are ready for action. Turn the cup upside down.

Watch your robot create wiggly designs across the paper. Jazzy!

BZZZZ!

8 Glue the motor to the bottom of the cup, using the hot glue gun. Connect the motor to the batteries. Remove the caps from the markers. Place the robot on a large sheet of white paper. Switch on the motor.

HOW IT WORKS

Many scientific instruments, such as earthquake detectors, use a pen to trace their findings. Here, the movements of the penbot are recorded by the marker tips running over the paper. The movement is created by the off-center cam (the washer) and is surprisingly random!

WALKABOUT BOT

YOU WILL NEED:

Not quite Frankenstein's monster (we hope)—but this is one Godzilla of a bot once its pulleys and motor are up and running (or at least walking). Make way!

TOOLS:
- Compass
- Utility knife
- White glue
- Clothespins
- Hot glue gun
- Craft drill
- Wire cutters
- Needle-nose pliers
- Scissors

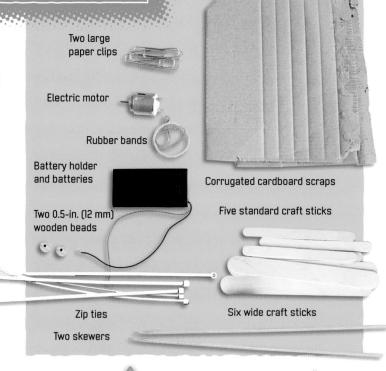

Two large paper clips

Electric motor

Rubber bands

Battery holder and batteries

Two 0.5-in. (12 mm) wooden beads

Zip ties

Two skewers

Corrugated cardboard scraps

Five standard craft sticks

Six wide craft sticks

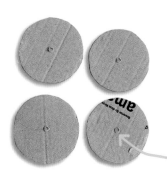

1 For the two pulleys, draw then cut out eight cardboard discs with a utility knife: four 1.8 in. (45 mm) and four 2 in. (50 mm) in diameter. Pierce the centers with a skewer.

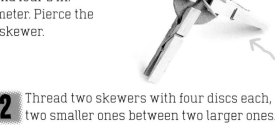

2 Thread two skewers with four discs each, two smaller ones between two larger ones. Glue them together with white glue, and clamp them with clothespins until the glue is dry.

3 Choose a rubber band to fit easily around each pulley. Trim one skewer to 2.8 in. (70 mm) and the other to 3.5 in. (90 mm) using scissors, a utility knife, or wire cutters.

4 Use a hot glue gun to attach the motor to a wide craft stick just off center, as shown. Make sure it is as straight as possible.

5 Drill skewer-sized holes in two wide craft sticks, as shown, 1.6 in. (40 mm) apart. Cut out two cardboard washers the width of the craft sticks.

6 Assemble the parts as shown to make this gearbox. The skewers should hold the craft sticks 2 in. (50 mm) apart. The wide crosswise sticks are 0.4 in. (10 mm) apart. Hold the gearbox together with hot glue.

Add the washers to the ends of the upper skewer. When the glue is dry, trim the ends off the crosswise sticks with scissors, a utility knife, or wire cutters.

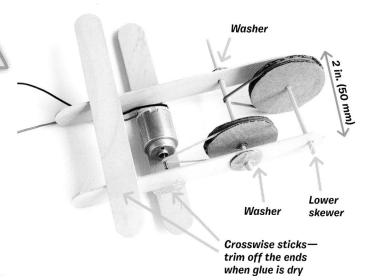

Washer

2 in. (50 mm)

Washer

Lower skewer

Crosswise sticks—trim off the ends when glue is dry

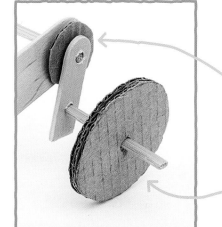

7 To make the two crank handles, cut two 1.4-in. (35 mm) pieces of standard craft stick, and drill skewer-sized holes near each end. Make two 0.6-in. (15 mm) cardboard washers.

Use white glue to glue a washer and craft stick on each end of the lower skewer, so they point in opposite directions. Insert and glue a 1.6-in. (40 mm) skewer length into the other hole and add two 1.2-in. (30 mm) washers on either side.

8 To make the two crank arms, drill ⚠ skewer-sized holes in two wide craft sticks, 3 in. (80 mm) apart. Cut the other end square.

9 Straighten out a paper clip with pliers and make a hook at one end. Add on a bead at the other end and bend the wire at a right angle. Repeat with another paper clip and bead.

Crank handles point in opposite directions.

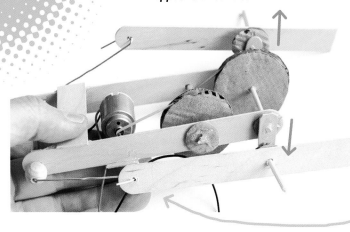

10 Thread the crank arms onto the lower skewers on the gearbox, as shown. Connect the arms to the top of the gearbox using the shaped paper clips. Fold over the top ends of the wires to hold the beads in place.

11 Stand the machine upright and glue on two standard craft sticks with white glue, as shown.

12 Cut one end off four standard craft sticks with a utility knife or wire cutters. Glue them flat below each end of the lengthwise sticks, as shown.

13 Attach the battery holder between the crosswise sticks with zip ties and trim the ends with scissors. Connect the battery to the motor.

Keep back as your Walkabout Bot lumbers across the room!

CLIP
CLOP

CLIP
CLOP

REAL-WORLD ENGINEERING

Walking is an amazingly complex thing to do because it involves dozens of muscles pulling different ways at the same time. It takes small children months to develop the skills! This model cheats a bit by using supports across the feet to keep the model upright as it stands on one foot.

GLOSSARY

AUTOMATON

A machine or mechanism designed to follow a series of operations, named after the Greek word meaning "acting of your own will." It often mimics human or animal movements. Automata (the plural) have existed since ancient times and often seem to work independently. Examples are roaring lions, singing birds, an eighteenth-century "Digesting Duck" that both ate and pooped, cuckoo clocks, and props for magic shows. Before the arrival of clockwork, they were powered by water or wind and were often pieces of highly skilled engineering.

ELECTRICAL CIRCUIT

A path along which electrons from a source of electric current flow. The path is closed at both ends, making it a loop. The elements needed are the source (such as a battery), a conductor (such as copper wire), a load (such as a light bulb or buzzer that shows the circuit is turned on), and an on/off switch.

CAM

A shaped wheel that rotates on an axle. It is used to convert a rotational (turning) motion into linear (straightforward) motion—or vice versa.

CENTER OF GRAVITY

An imaginary point in an object where its total weight is thought to be concentrated: that is, where the force of gravity appears to act. In a symmetrical object, it is located at the geometric center; in an asymmetrical object, it will be off-center. In humans, this will be roughly in front of the lower vertebrae but varies according to position.

FULCRUM

The support on which a lever turns to raise or move something.

KINETIC ENERGY

The energy that all moving objects have. The amount depends on an object's mass and speed.

LEVER

A rigid bar or beam that pivots on a fulcrum. It transforms forces, making them act in new ways. The simplest lever will change the direction of a force. By adjusting the position of the fulcrum, a small force applied over a large distance can be converted to a large force acting over a small distance. This is how a crowbar can lift a heavy object. The Greek mathematician Archimedes wrote about levers and made them their own branch of physics. He said that if you gave him a long enough lever and a place to stand, he could move the Earth!

PROSTHETIC

An artificial body part, such as a limb or hand, that replaces one lost. Prosthetic limbs are designed to work and move as naturally and efficiently as possible. The science of prosthetics is very ancient, and one Egyptian mummy was found to have a wooden prosthetic toe.

ROTATIONAL INERTIA

The force that opposes the tendency of something to rotate. In the case of tightrope walkers, they have to position themselves in a way that keeps the wire from rotating and tipping them off. Spreading out their mass by carrying a balancing pole helps tightrope walkers to do this.

INDEX

THE AUTHOR

Rob Ives is a former math and science teacher who is currently a designer and paper engineer living in Cumbria, UK. He creates science- and project-based children's books, including *Paper Models that Rock!* and *Paper Automata*. He specializes in character-based paper animations and all kinds of fun and fascinating science projects, and he often visits schools to talk about design technology and to demonstrate his models. Rob's other series for Hungry Tomato include *Tabletop Battles* and *Amazing Science Experiments*.

Picture Credits
(abbreviations: t = top; b = bottom; c = center; l = left; r = right)
Shutterstock.com: Dean Drobot 9br; Designua 19bl; Dim Dimich 6tr, 13br & 31cr; globalmoments 29bl; Katoosha 16br & 30br.

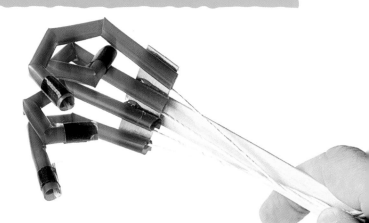